30+ FRACTAL ARTWORKS

ADULT COLORING BOOK

VOL. I

COLOR TESTING

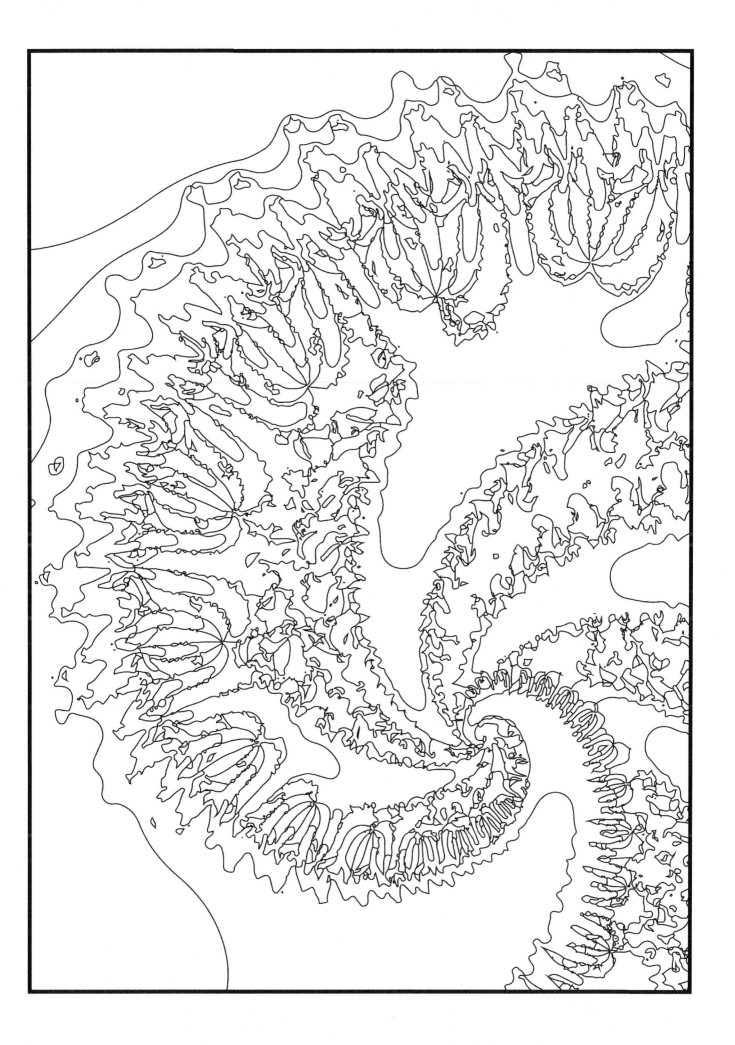

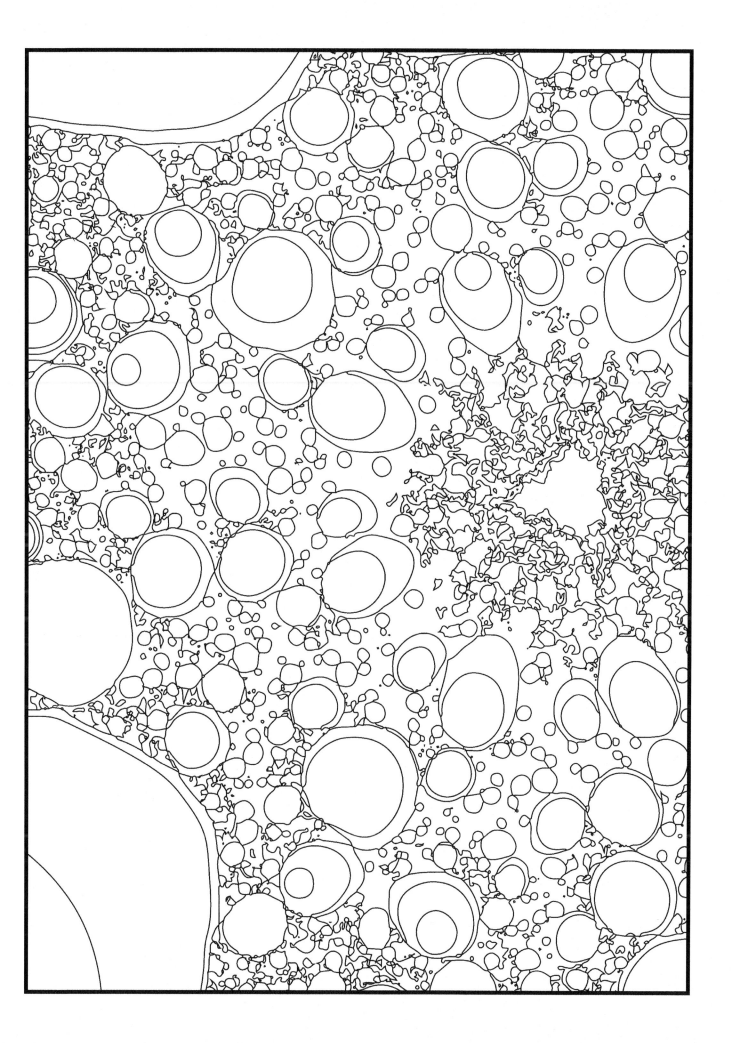

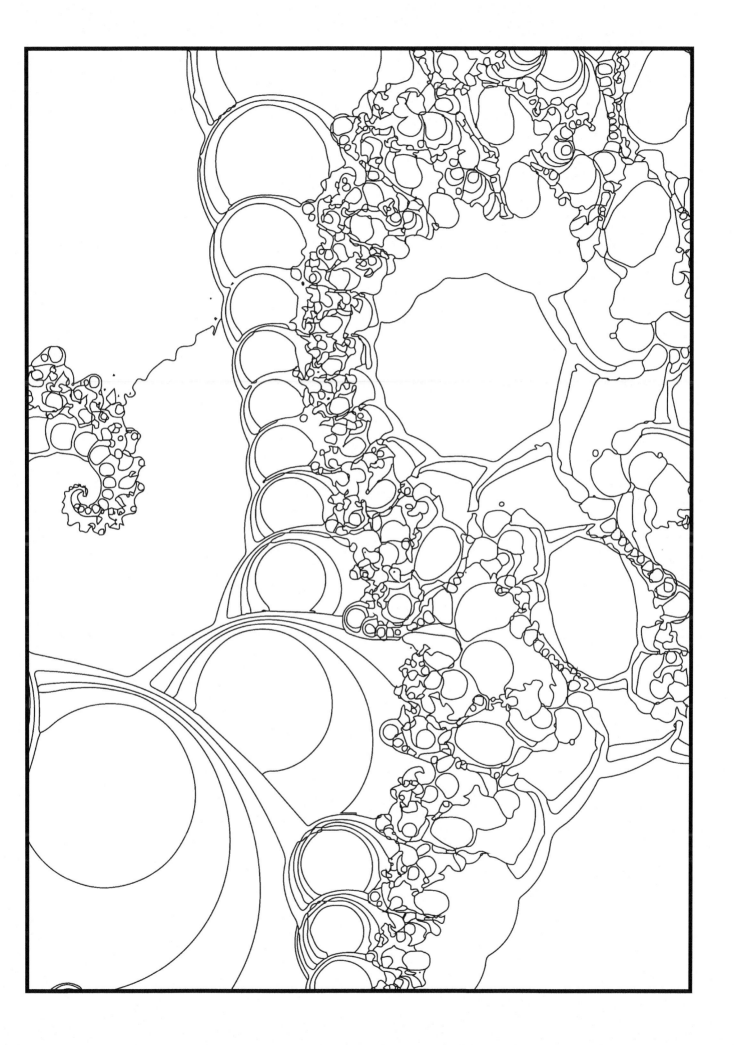

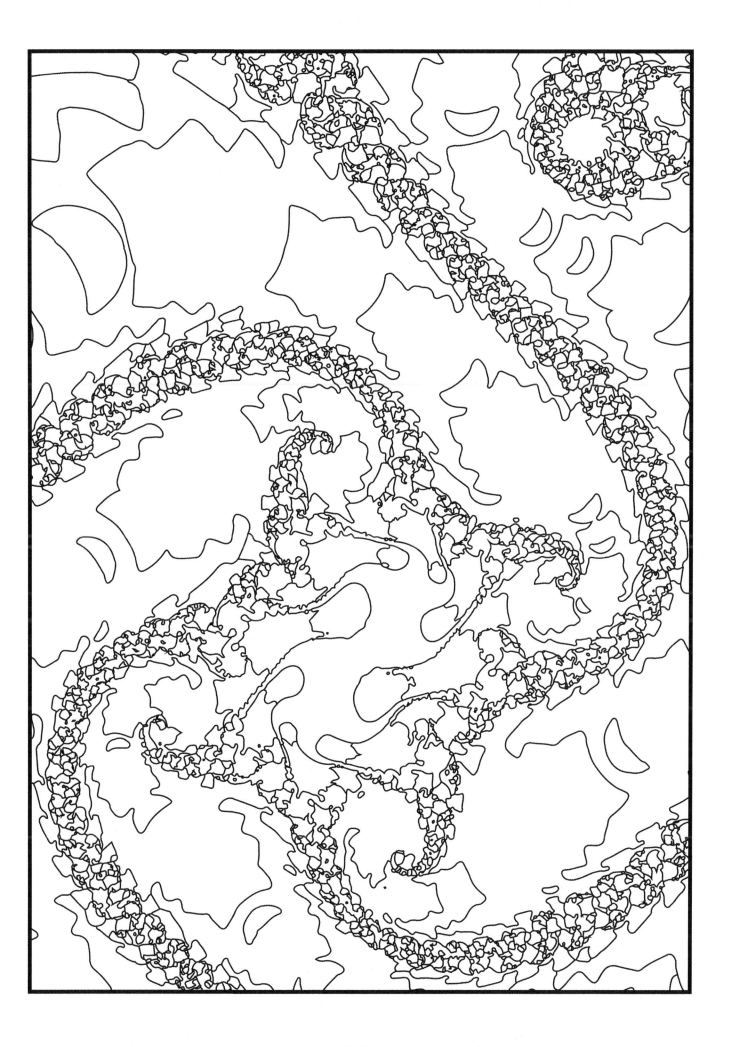

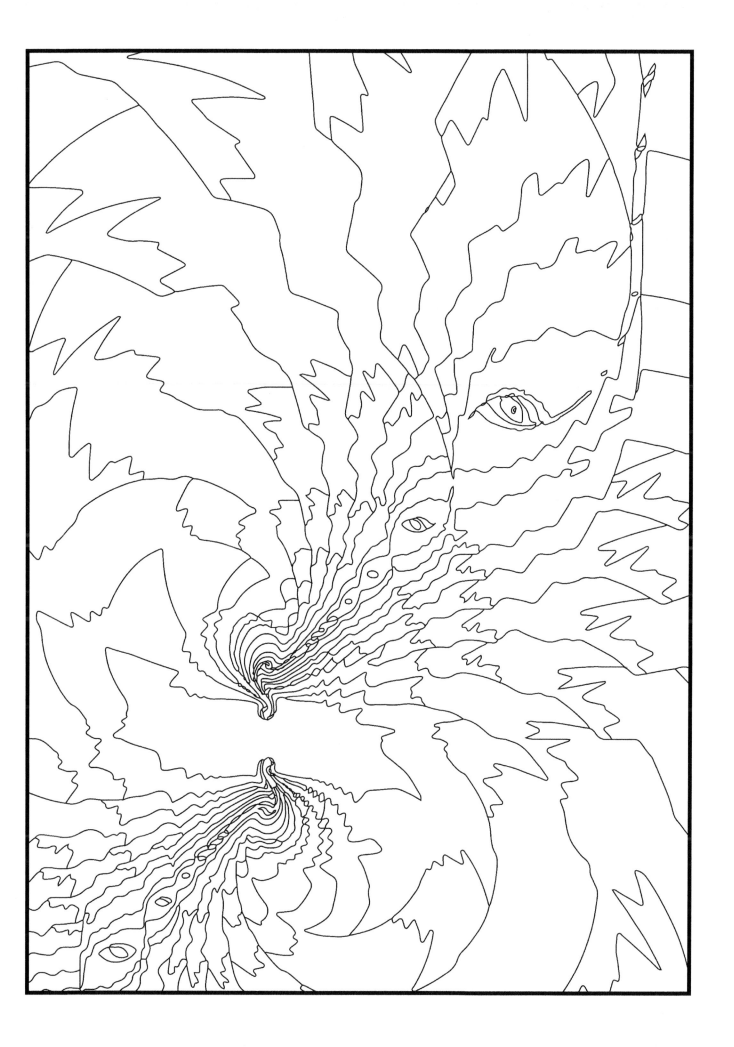

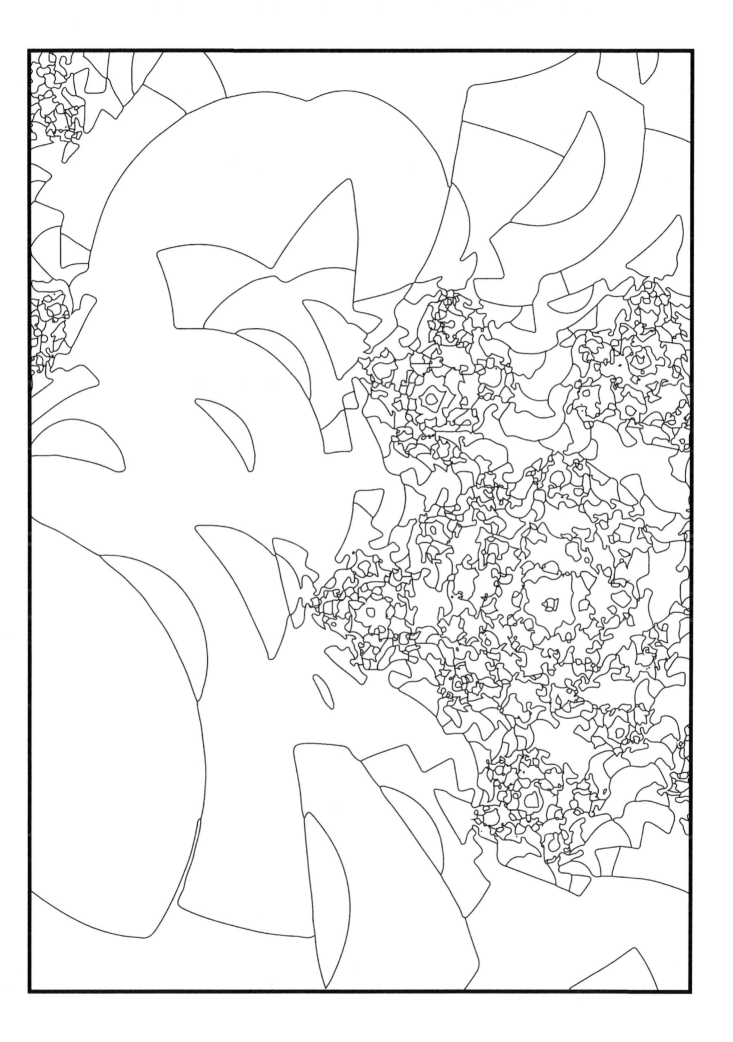

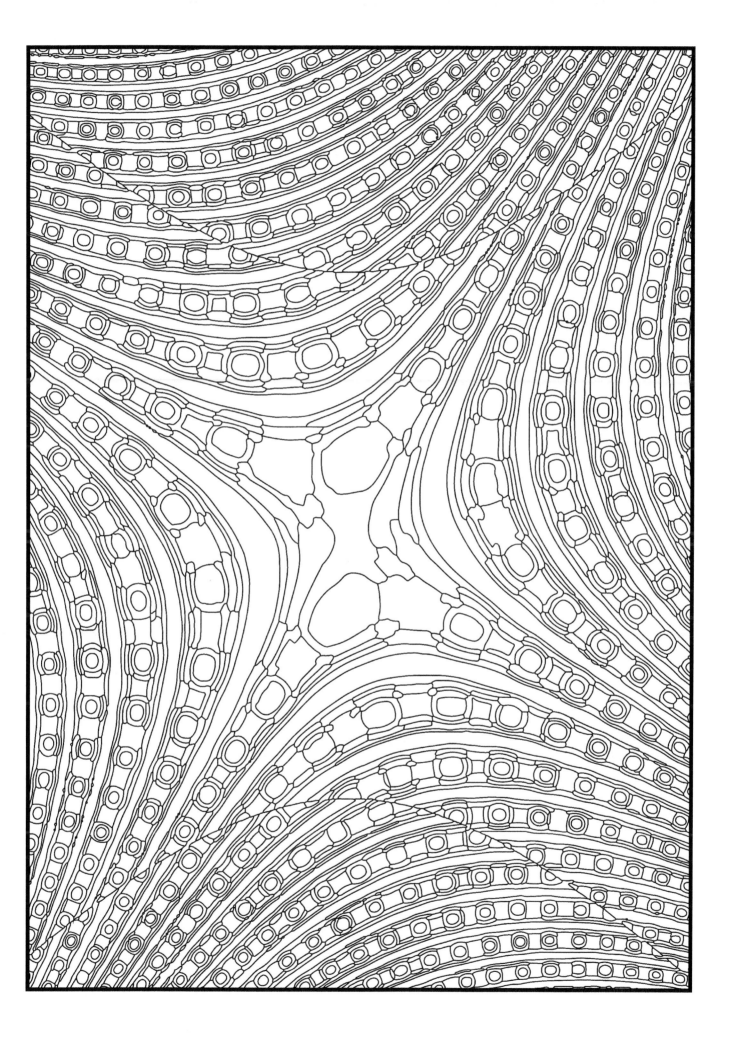

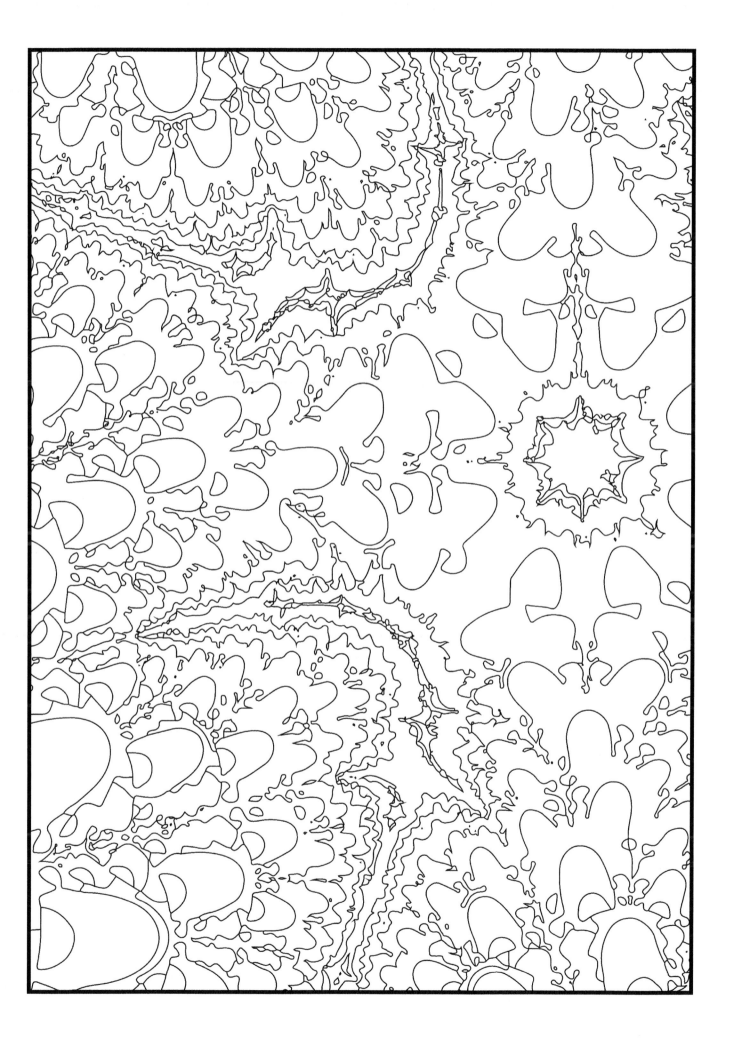

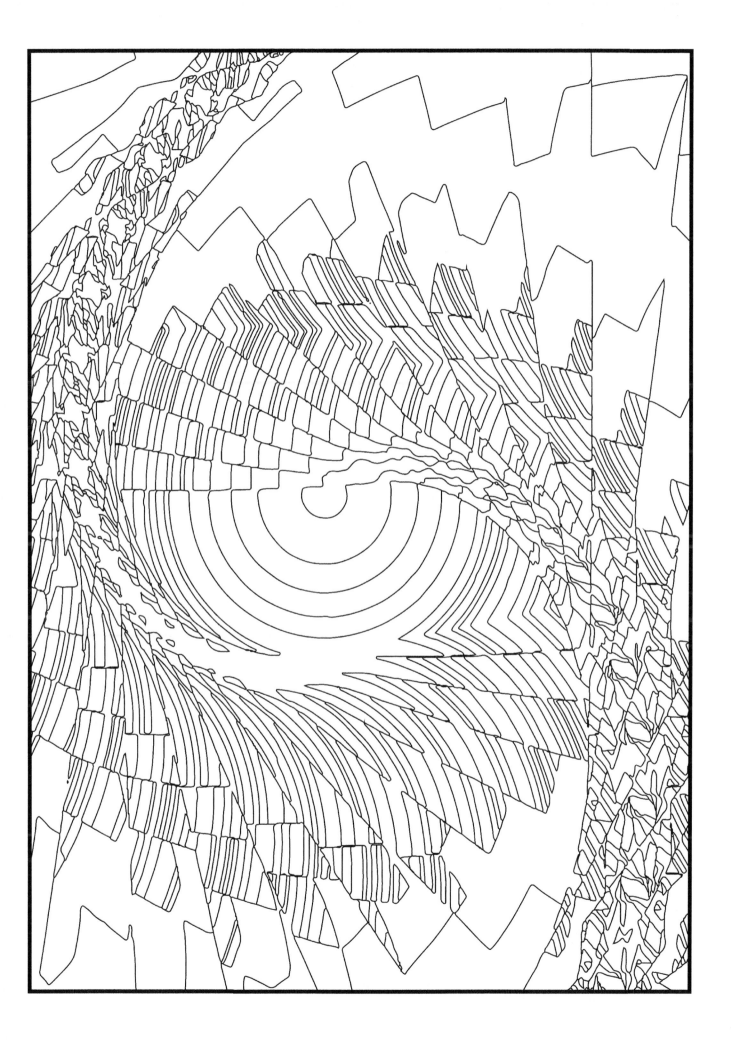

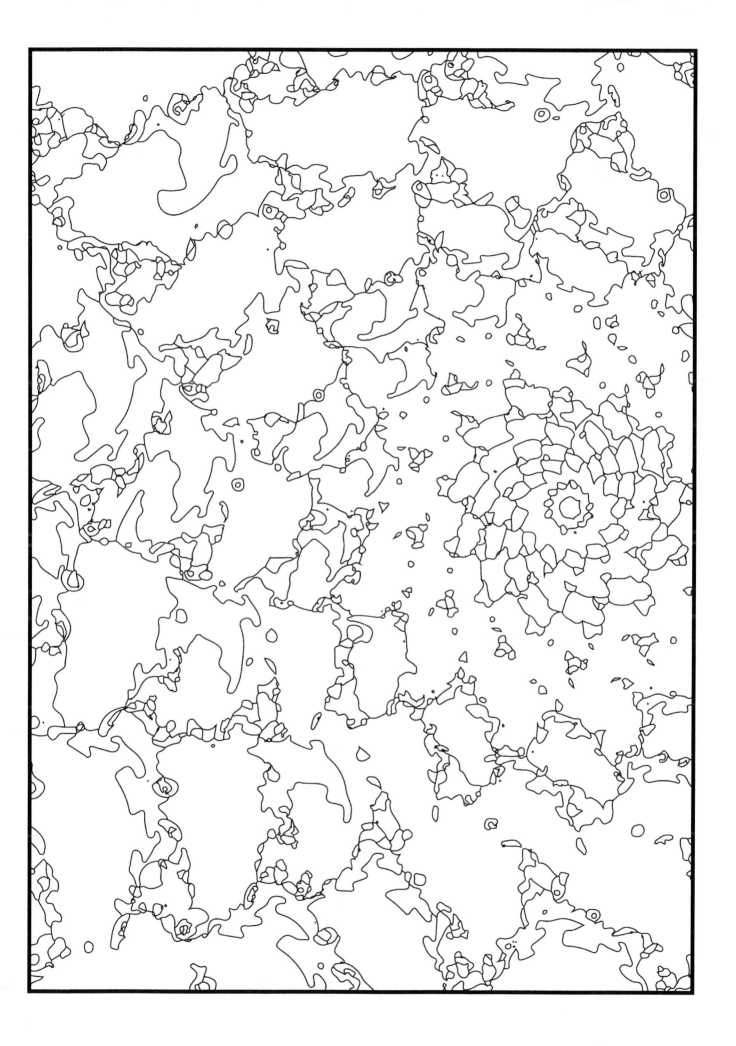

Printed in Great Britain
by Amazon

81219948R00041

Where, oh where is Summer's fluffy cat?

Is she on the sofa under mummy's pink hat?

She likes to go where people once sat.

She likes the warmth; could this be where she is hiding at?

I fed her this morning, have a look by the cat flap.

Sometimes she stays there waiting for scraps.

After Her food she becomes a lazy cat;

she'll take a quick nap.

She's usually upstairs under your bed.

She likes to go where you lay down your head.

I don't know why she doesn't use her cat shed.

We have searched all over for
Summer's fluffy cat.
We went up, down, left and right.
North, South, East and West.

Use the Compass to help you point in the direction we found Mittens.
(Mittens was upstairs)

Well done! Mittens was North because she was upstairs.

Use the compass to help you point in the opposite direction to North.

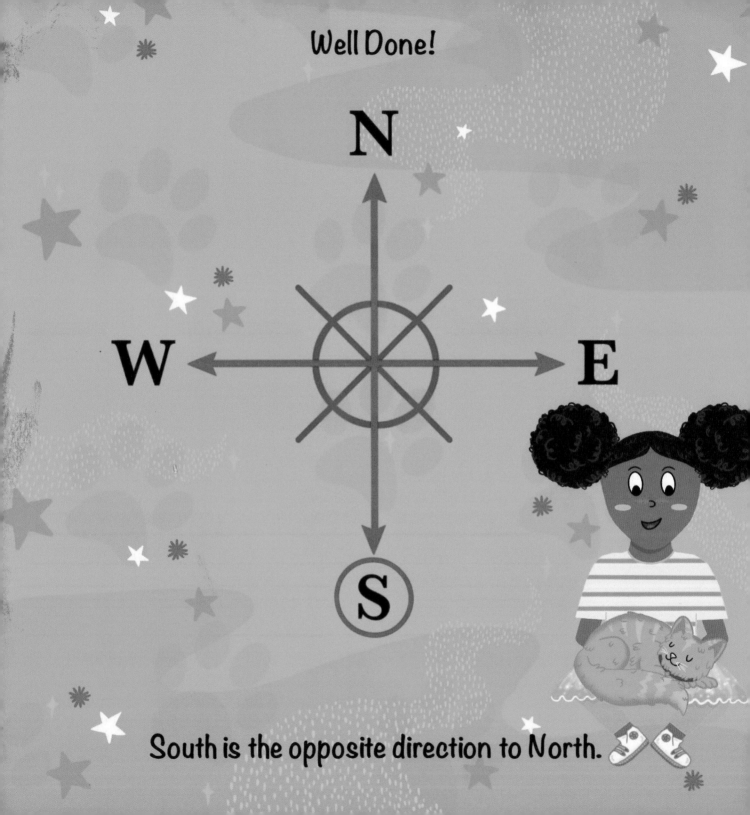

Well Done!

South is the opposite direction to North.

Thanks for helping us find Mittens :)

Goodbye for now!

(See you soon...)

S A B C D E F G H

I L L

L n o P

Q E R

S t g

r n

t y r

ot coco New

Love For

Pixie

m

Printed in Poland
by Amazon Fulfillment
Poland Sp. z o.o., Wrocław

63422794R00016